How To Use This Study Guide

This five-lesson study guide corresponds to *"Breaking Hell's Economy" With Rick Renner and Joseph Z* **(Renner TV)**. Each lesson in this study guide covers a topic that is addressed during the program series, with questions and references supplied to draw you deeper into your own private study of the Scriptures on this subject.

To derive the most benefit from this study guide, consider the following:

First, watch or listen to the program prior to working through the corresponding lesson in this guide. (Programs can also be viewed at **renner.org** by clicking on the Media/Archives links or on our Renner Ministries YouTube channel.)

Second, take the time to look up the scriptures included in each lesson. Prayerfully consider their application to your own life.

Third, use a journal or notebook to make note of your answers to each lesson's Study Questions and Practical Application challenges.

Fourth, invest specific time in prayer and in the Word of God to consult with the Holy Spirit. Write down the scriptures or insights He reveals to you.

Finally, take action! Whatever the Lord tells you to do according to His Word, do it.

For added insights on this subject, it is recommended that you obtain Joseph Z's book ***Breaking Hell's Economy: Your Guide to Last-Days Supernatural Provision***. You may also select from Rick's other available resources by placing your order at **renner.org** or by calling 1-800-742-5593.

TOPIC

A Collision of Systems

SYNOPSIS

The five lessons in this study titled **Breaking Hell's Economy** will focus on the following topics:

- A Collision of Systems
- What if the World Collapses?
- A Corporate Superpower
- A Future Without Babylon
- Breaking Hell's Economy Off Your Family

The emphasis of this lesson:

The kingdom of darkness and all its dealings are hell's economy, and this economy is railing against God's Kingdom of light. The only thing that can stand against the enemy's outlandish efforts and break hell's economy is the Kingdom of God.

What Is Hell's Economy?

When we talk about hell's economy, we're talking about the opposite of the Kingdom of God. The Kingdom of God is God's economy, and the Bible says, "…[It] is not eating and drinking, but righteousness and peace and joy in the Holy Spirit" (Romans 14:17 *NKJV*). God's Kingdom is an everlasting Kingdom where His rule is supreme.

In contrast is the kingdom of darkness — or hell's economy. Jesus called it "the gates of hell" (*see* Matthew 16:18), and it is in an explosive, head-to-head battle with God's Kingdom like never before. The only thing that can stand against darkness and break hell's economy is the Church of the Lord Jesus Christ. Jesus Himself declared, "…The gates of hell shall not prevail against it" (Matthew 16:18).

A Note From Rick Renner

I am on a personal quest to see a "revival of the Bible" so people can establish their lives on a firm foundation that will stand strong and endure the test as end-time storm winds begin to intensify.

In order to experience a revival of the Bible in your personal life, it is important to take time each day to read, receive, and apply its truths to your life. James tells us that if we will continue in the perfect law of liberty — refusing to be forgetful hearers, but determined to be doers — we will be blessed in our ways. As you watch or listen to the programs in this series and work through this corresponding study guide, I trust you will search the Scriptures and allow the Holy Spirit to help you hear something new from God's Word that applies specifically to your life. I encourage you to be a doer of the Word He reveals to you. Whatever the cost, I assure you — it will be worth it.

> Thy words were found, and I did eat them;
> and thy word was unto me the joy and rejoicing of mine heart:
> for I am called by thy name, O Lord God of hosts.
> —Jeremiah 15:16

Your brother and friend in Jesus Christ,

Rick Renner

Breaking Hell's Economy

Copyright © 2023 by Rick Renner

1814 W. Tacoma St.

Broken Arrow, OK 74012-1406

Published by Rick Renner Ministries

www.renner.org

ISBN 13: 978-1-6675-0373-8

eBook ISBN 13: 978-1-6675-0374-5

The New Testament word for "church" is *ekklesia*, and it means *the called-out ones.* It was taken from the Athenian culture, and it pictures a distinguished group of people who have been called out, called forth, selected, and assembled to be God's representatives in every town, city, state, or nation. Like the ancient *ekklesia* in Athens, the Church (*ekklesia*) is *a body called to make decisions that affect the atmosphere of a region.* God Himself is building the Church, and the gates of hell will not prevail against it!

A Clash of Two Kingdoms

Oftentimes, when a culture begins to sink into the mire of evil and depravity (like ours is currently), it's because the Church has been lulled to sleep by the enemy. It's at this time that God begins to call out to different people in the Church and urge them to rise, speak the truth, and stand for righteousness. It is this supernatural persistence and bulldog faith of God's people that break hell's economy, its power, and its influence.

Right now, we're living in a day when there is a clash of kingdoms — the kingdom of darkness is fighting fiercely against the Kingdom of light. We see evidence of this not just on the news, but also on our streets, in our schools, and in our communities every day. Unrighteousness is railing against righteousness, and although we've seen similar battles many times before, the situation has never seemed more all-encompassing than in the last few years.

The gates of hell are feverishly trying to take territory in all arenas: the political system, the financial system, the education system, the religious system, the social system, and even in the lives of our children. Although the Antichrist himself has not yet been unveiled and taken center stage, the dark institution (the global system that is driven by the spirit of antichrist), is determined to swallow up and re-orchestrate society to match its agenda.

Yet God is using the chaos to sound a wake-up call to the Church. In the midst of all the madness, He's urging His people who are called by His Name to step forward and boldly proclaim the truth. Just as the evil queen Jezebel tried to control the culture and silence the voice of God's people in the days of Elijah, the spirit of Jezebel has returned and is attempting to do the same today. But God is empowering His people to speak, pierce the veil of darkness, and push back against the gates of hell.

Insanity Is Being Celebrated

Joseph Z shared how what he calls "the pervert mafia" is proliferating and parading across the United States. Sheer lunacy and mental illness have become mainstream, and people are calling themselves anything they want to be. One person may say he is a turtle, and another identifies as a cat and demands litter boxes be placed in the public-school bathrooms. The saddest part of it all is that this insanity is celebrated, and whatever is celebrated and tolerated increases over time, which gives more place to the devil.

Clearly, we're living in the day described by the prophet Isaiah — a day when people "…call evil good, and good evil; Who put darkness for light, and light for darkness; Who put bitter for sweet, and sweet for bitter! (Isaiah 5:20 *NKJV*).

Again, the only thing that can stand against these outlandish efforts of the kingdom of darkness and break hell's economy is the Kingdom of God. As God's people, we need a supernatural boldness to empower us to rise up and push back against all the craziness.

Some people are afraid to stand up and speak out. They're afraid they'll be mistreated and categorized as a bigot or "phobe" of some kind. Yet there comes a time when you've got to set fear aside, open your mouth and call what's wrong, wrong and what's right, right. As the Church, it is crucial that we speak the truth of God's Word, so we can maintain our position of spiritual authority.

We Are Called Out To Represent Christ

The book of Exodus records God's supernatural rescue of the nation of Israel out of Egyptian bondage. Before God delivered His people, He demonstrated His mighty superiority over the gods of Egypt through ten plagues — the ninth one being a plague of darkness (*see* Exodus 10).

During that time, the Israelites were living in the land of Goshen, which is in the Nile Delta on the right branch of the river. Amazingly, while deep darkness covered Egypt, the area of Goshen was shining with light. Imagine it: As the Egyptians sat paralyzed in darkness so thick it could be felt, God's people were beaming with light!

As God's people, we've seen a great deal of darkness in the last few years, and while we're not living near the Nile, many Christians are in de-nile (denial). In other words, they're not believing in and trusting God to keep His promises. The truth is that just as He supernaturally provided the Israelites with light in the midst of darkness, His light will arise and shine upon His people today!

We are the *ekklesia* — the Church of the Lord Jesus Christ. We are the called-out ones created to shine His light in the middle of an extremely dark culture. That's why God said, "Arise, my people! Let your light shine for all the nations to see! For the glory of the Lord is streaming from you. Darkness as black as night shall cover all the peoples of the earth, but the glory of the Lord will shine from you. All nations will come to your light; mighty kings will come to see the glory of the Lord upon you" (Isaiah 60:1-3 *TLB*).

The traditional media that has been covering our country and the world for years is more or less a legacy media. Many people, believers included, have become accustomed to sitting back and swallowing everything mainstream media dishes out. The problem is that what they're dishing out today is almost all poisonous. From the tragedy of transgenderism to the staged protests to focusing on negative news and nonstop attacks against good people, legacy media has little, if any, value whatsoever. Their efforts to stun and desensitize viewers have unfortunately caused countless people to become so numb to the depravity of our culture that we embrace it as normal out of sheer exhaustion.

There are people everywhere — including many unbelievers — who are deeply unnerved by all that we see happening, and they're asking questions. God has the answers, and He is speaking to them through us, His Church. The information about the end times is not meant to scare us but to prepare us. But to be prepared, we have to understand who we are in Christ and how He's positioned us in this hour to break hell's economy.

God Has a Secret Weapon Up His Sleeve

Guess what that secret weapon is? It's us! It's His Church. We are the light in darkness. Christ in us is the hope of glory (*see* Colossians 1:27).

In this seemingly overwhelming season, we need a right-now word from the Lord. The perversity being paraded and celebrated is not normal, right, or producing anything good. It is destroying people's lives, and if we really love people the way Jesus tells us to, we have the privilege *and* responsibility to learn how to treat them the way He does and speak the truth in love without fear.

Many believers have heard that it's *the anointing that breaks the yoke of bondage*, and while this is certainly true, there is more to this verse that needs to be understood. The Bible says:

> **It shall come to pass in that day that his burden will be taken away from your shoulder, and his yoke from your neck, and the yoke will be destroyed because of the *anointing* oil.**
>
> **— Isaiah 10:27 (*NKJV*)**

The "anointing" described here is a Hebrew word that means *fatness* or *muscularity for growth*. What's interesting is that this passage reveals three levels of anointing that operate in a person's life. The first level is the anointing that causes the burden to be lifted off someone's shoulder. The second is the anointing that loosens the neck, and the third level is an anointing that destroys the yoke completely.

These levels of anointing also illustrate three levels of blessing and advancement. The first level, when the weight of bondage is lifted off the shoulders, is the *thirty-fold blessing*. This is where believers think, *I'm free! I've never felt freedom like this before.* Unfortunately, many Christians stop there and settle for much less than God's best.

Then there are others who believe God for more, and they experience a greater anointing that loosens their neck. This is like the *sixty-fold* level of breakthrough, where individuals that were bound can stretch and freely look around. And because they feel lighter and their vision has expanded, some tend to settle there, but that's not God's best either.

The third level of anointing is the *hundred-fold* level. It is the breakthrough anointing that lifts the heaviness off the shoulders, loosens the neck to move freely with greater vision, and destroys the yoke of bondage completely. This level of breakthrough anointing is God's very best, and He desires all His people to experience it.

An anointing of this nature enables one to outgrow his yoke or containment. It's the kind of supernatural power God's people need to break hell's economy — to break the back of the kingdom of darkness. It's the kind of anointing that ignites a supernatural passion in people to rise up and say, "This evil and perversity are not going to happen today, not on my watch! We will take back what the enemy has stolen and no longer be intimidated by any demonic darkness."

Friend, we are God's secret weapon, and we need His supernatural anointing to come upon us and infuse us with a righteous indignation. Now, this is not a carnal anger energized by selfishness or fear. It is a holy, godly anger against unrighteousness that moves us to take a stand against the bullying spirit of Jezebel that is trying to silence God's voice and sanitize society of every trace of His image.

There's Nothing New Under the Sun

Do you remember how Jezebel was killed during the days of Elijah? The Bible says it was the eunuchs — the men who had been surgically emasculated — that grabbed Jezebel and threw her out of the palace window where she was run over by a chariot. This is a picture of what could very well happen in our day.

Joseph Z said, "I believe God is looking to bring revival to those bound by sexual perversity — even those in the vice grips of transgenderism. As this perverted generation is awakened by God and they repent and get saved, they will turn from darkness to light. And I sense the breakthrough He brings is going to offend institutional minds."

Ecclesiastes 1:9 (*ESV*) says, "What has been is what will be, and what has been done is what will be done, and there is nothing new under the sun." Believe it or not, this is true of transgenderism. A careful study of history reveals that in the city of Smyrna in the First Century, there was a cult called Cybele, and it was made up of trans women. In fact, the only way you could be a priestess in the cult of Cybele was if you had first been a man and then had your male organs removed and your body enhanced to appear as a woman. The saying in the city was you always knew who the priestesses were because they were the most beautiful women in Smyrna.

This means the Early Church had to deal with the issue of transgenderism, and if they were empowered to deal with it, so are we. God wants people who are struggling with deep pain and their self-image to have their eyes opened, discover how much He loves them, and turn back towards Him to receive His abundant grace and salvation.

Real Love Tells the Truth

The Bible says, "…The love of God has been poured out in our hearts by the Holy Spirit who was given to us" (Romans 5:5 *NKJV*). Through the power of the Holy Spirit, we can love every broken person that is lost and separated from God. It is the lovingkindness of the Lord working through us that draws the unsaved to Jesus.

Now, the love of God is not the same as the love of the world. Real love from God speaks the truth in a kind yet firm way. Real love calls sin, sin AND shows genuine compassion for the one trapped in bondage. Real love listens to people's stories to hear their heart's condition and helps walk them through repentance and deliverance in order to be restored. Any preacher or believer that doesn't lovingly speak the truth to a dying generation, doesn't fully love people.

Think about it. If a person sees a child running across the street into traffic and says, "Ah, that's just so pitiful. That child is going to get hit by a car and killed." That's not real love. Real love — the God-kind of love — turns to the child heading for life-threatening danger and screams, "Stop! Don't go there! You're going to get hurt!" Real love tells the truth to try to save people from death.

Jude 1:23 tells us that real love reaches into the fires of destruction to pull people out. Actions like these are a part of breaking hell's economy. In these last-of-the-last days, God wants to bring together a corporate anointing. This type of anointing is symbolized in Scripture by the gates of Zion, and God loves the gates of Zion more than all the dwellings of Jacob.

Psalm 87 reveals that the gates of Zion represent the gathering place of believers where all the people came together to celebrate the gates of the city. In contrast, the dwellings of Jacob represent individual family gatherings where people come together at their campfires and celebrate with their tribe.

The corporate gathering is what we've been missing in the Body of Christ. It has profound power and is something God truly loves. Together, we're a corporate superpower, and we can influence this culture. That's the Church. We're called to stand against the gates of hell and influence every part of culture.

STUDY QUESTIONS

**Study to shew thyself approved unto God, a workman that
needeth not to be ashamed, rightly dividing the word of truth.**
— 2 Timothy 2:15

1. There are so many parallels between these last-of-the-last days and
   the days of Elijah and Jezebel. Take a look at First Kings 18. What
   stands out most to you about Elijah? How about Obadiah, Jezebel,
   and her entourage? What do you notice about how God responds to
   Elijah's faith and obedience?

2. Real love tells the truth, even when it's not popular and very painful
   to acknowledge and deal with. What hard but necessary truth did
   Nathan have to tell David out of love in Second Samuel 12? How did
   David respond? (*See* Psalm 51.)

PRACTICAL APPLICATION

**But be ye doers of the word, and not hearers only,
deceiving your own selves.**
—James 1:22

1. What did you imagine the last days would be like? How did you think
   they would affect you personally? What has this lesson shown you
   about God's mindfulness of you and His will for you in the middle of
   such crazy times?

2. Can you remember a time when someone confronted you out of
   genuine love and concern for you, after earning the right to speak into
   your life? What did they say to you? How did you respond? Do you
   wish you'd done anything differently?

3. What's one sin or issue that's caused a lot of hurt in your own life
   (or someone else's) that you have a passion to help people gain and
   maintain freedom? Ask God to help you have discernment to know
   when and how to speak the truth in love to people when they're
   struggling with sin of all kinds (not just sexual), and how to respond
   out of His heart for them, not out of a need to be right.

TOPIC

What if the World Collapses?

SYNOPSIS

Jesus said that one of the signs of the last days would be *famines* in various places (*see* Matthew 24:7). When most people hear this, they think it has to do with crop failures and food shortages, and while it certainly does include scarcity of food, there's something else important that Jesus is telling us.

During the First Century, most economies were based on the quantity of grain in a country's possession. It's kind of like a nation's strength in the trading of commodities in the stock market today. Jesus and the audience He was speaking to were aware of this. Thus, when He said there will be famines, He wasn't just prophesying a shortage of food — He was also prophesying financial crises in the markets of the world.

Look around you. That is exactly what we're seeing. We're living in a day of rollercoaster markets — up one moment and down the next. We're even seeing an increase in the collapse of banks and the currency of certain countries. No one really knows what's going to happen next — but God! In the midst of this increasing instability, the voice of the prophet Isaiah is growing louder: "Seek the Lord while He may be found, Call upon Him while He is near" (Isaiah 55:6 *NKJV*).

The emphasis of this lesson:

Without question, the world's systems are on the brink of a catastrophic collapse. Satan is behind the scenes, pulling the strings to manipulate his one-world order into place. But don't fear. God is on the job and has us — His people — in place. The Church and the Gospel are the answer in these troubling times.

Satan Is the Master Manipulator

Think about it. All the world's systems — including the global economy — are basically built on a Babylonian, Tower-of-Babel mindset. "Come," the leaders shouted, "Let us make a name for ourselves…" (*see* Genesis 11:4). Just as the people were motivated to do things their way and disregard God's instructions, the subconscious, cultural mentality is much the same today: elevate self and eliminate God from every sphere of society.

Behind it all is the master manipulator, Satan. He doesn't have the anointing of God's Holy Spirit, so he manipulates people, situations, and the world's systems to accomplish his goals. The Bible says he's the "god of this world" (2 Corinthians 4:4), and the word "world" in this verse is the Greek word *kosmos*, which describes *the organized systems of the world.* This would include the systems of education, entertainment, world markets, finances, the courts, and religion. Thus, *Satan is the god of systems.*

Like a marionette puppeteer, Satan knows the right strings to pull at just the right time and in just the right order to get the people under his control to do exactly what he wants. But guess what? Even though he's a master manipulator of systems, we as believers have the power to *override* the system! First John 5:4 says, "For whatsoever is born of God overcometh the world: and this is the victory that overcometh the world, even our faith." Interestingly, the word "world" in this verse is again the Greek word *kosmos*, which describes *the organized systems of the world.*

This same verse in *The Message* Bible says, "Every God-born person conquers the world's ways. The conquering power that brings the world to its knees is our faith." Friend, the power that defies the world systems is our faith. The Holy Spirit infuses us with His anointing to override the system and all the propaganda the enemy is promoting on the world's stage.

A System on the Brink of Collapse

Many prophetic voices right now are sensing and saying that the world's system is on the brink of a catastrophic collapse, and that is true. We're seeing it happening all around us in ways we'd never imagined. Even the unsaved are feeling a sense of alarm as they see things they used to trust in coming apart at the seams. Many are saying, "What in the world is going on? Is there any recovery from all that we are experiencing?"

At the same time, there are some people saying, "Oh, everything's going to be fine," but that's not true. There are very real challenges we're dealing with and still others we have yet to face. Still, that doesn't mean we have to be afraid or shrink back in silence. On the contrary, out of this tragedy can come great triumph. Indeed, this is the finest hour for every believer to be alive.

"But what if the world collapses?" some are asking. "What if the *kosmos* or the world systems actually unravel and fall apart?" Well, first, the world itself and human life are never going to end. It will, however, transition into a new season. Right now, we're living in what many refer to as the Church Age. When it ends at the time of the Rapture, the Day of the Lord — also known as the Tribulation and the Wrath of the Lamb — will begin. This will be followed by the Millennial reign of Christ and then the new heavens and the new earth — all of which are described in the book of Revelation.

When we talk about the collapse of the world, we are referring to the failure of *man-made* systems. What's interesting is that there is a definite pattern or cycle we can see through history. In the time of Noah, which was approximately 1,650 years after creation, there was a worldwide cataclysmic collapse. But God preserved humanity in the lives of the eight that were in the ark and rebooted the world after the Flood. Another collapse took place when Egypt held the role as the world's superpower. Amid an unprecedented famine, God positioned Joseph to save the world from starvation.

Again and again, world systems have been built and collapsed, but the world eventually went on. Likewise, amid the moral meltdown of society today and the crumbling economies of the world, God is actively on the job, and He will bring His people through. Even now, He's raising up His Church to be a light in darkness and a voice of truth in an age of deception. It's as if we're watching a real-life action movie, and the hero being raised up is the Spirit of God coming alive in the Church.

So, even if the systems of the world collapse, don't panic. God has His people purposefully positioned across the planet — we are modern-day Noahs, Josephs, and Esthers, and we have been born for such a time as this! Although no one human being has the answer, God has it, and He's alive and active in us. That answer is the Church and the Gospel of Jesus Christ.

Tag — You're It!

Did you ever play tag as a kid? Well, in the game of tag, if the person who was "it" touched you, they would say, "Tag! You're it!" Then suddenly, you would be the most active one in the game, reaching out to tag others. Considering all the abounding signs around us, it is as if the Holy Spirit reached out and touched our generation and said, "Tag! You're it! Somebody has to be the end-time generation, and you guys are it."

Make no mistake — the fact that you're alive in this day and age is no accident. The Bible says, "…[God] made from one [common origin, one source, one blood] all nations of men to settle on the face of the earth, having definitely determined [their] allotted periods of time and the fixed boundaries of their habitation (their settlements, lands, and abodes)" (Acts 17:26 *AMPC*). What this means is that **you are anointed by God to live in these times**.

Just as Mordecai told Esther, the Holy Spirit is telling you, "…You have come to the kingdom for such a time as this and for this very occasion" (Esther 4:14 *AMPC*). Just imagine! You are seeing what the prophets prophesied about thousands of years ago. Indeed, it is an amazing time to be alive!

Seize the Day!

If we were to travel back in time to the early 1920s, we would see that the United States and many countries in the world were experiencing a time of great prosperity and celebration. It was an era known as the Roaring Twenties, and life was grand. But right at the end of that decade, in 1929, there came an unexpected collapse of the world's economy. In October of that year, the Great Depression began and launched millions of people into a terrible time of devastation. Although it lasted for about 25 years, those times came to an end, and the people came through it.

Although you don't hear too much about it, there were unique opportunities that popped up during those days — opportunities to position oneself for greatness and really move forward in the world. As strange as it may seem, similar opportunities are going to present themselves to us in our generation, even during great darkness.

Consider what took place in the Early Church. Acts 11:27 and 28 (*NLT*) says, "During this time some prophets traveled from Jerusalem to Antioch. One of them named Agabus stood up in one of the meetings and predicted by the Spirit that a great famine was coming upon the entire Roman world. (This was fulfilled during the reign of Claudius.)"

Notice this was a prophet of God that brought a *negative* word. Rather than verbally assault this messenger for having a negative confession or "bind the famine" from taking place, the Bible says, "…The believers in Antioch decided to send relief to the brothers and sisters in Judea, everyone giving as much as they could" (Acts 11:29 *NLT*).

Here we see these believers received the prophetic word as being directly from Heaven, and they prepared for what was coming. When the opportunity arrived, they seized it and became a blessing to fellow believers in need and brought God so much glory we're still talking about it 2,000 years later! Wow! What a demonstration of the purpose of prophecy. In God's great love, He reveals future events before they take place — not to scare us but to prepare us to do and be part of great things.

Think about what Jesus told the church of Smyrna in Revelation 2:10. He said, "Fear none of those things which thou shalt suffer…." Notice, He didn't say, "Bind the suffering that will try to come on you," or "Run from it." He simply told them it was coming, and He empowered them to make it through it.

The same holds true for us. In these last-of-the-last days, we're going to see some things that are very disturbing. The Bible calls these times "perilous" in Second Timothy 3:1, which in the Greek indicates that there's no way around them. It's just part of the territory that comes with the last days. But don't be afraid — it's okay. We're going to make it because the Greater One lives in us (*see* 1 John 4:4). We have the promises of His Word, and through the mighty power of the Holy Spirit, we're going to sail through victoriously because we are the blood-bought Bride of Jesus Christ! We can make it *and* break hell's economy at the same time.

A 'Now Word' for Our Generation

Joseph Z shared a prophetic, *now* word that the Holy Spirit revealed to him recently. He said that as he was standing by a body of water, he looked up and saw an eagle flying overhead. As he stood there watching the eagle, he said, "Lord, what is this about?" Then just as he was about to begin taking a video of the eagle to show his wife, Heather, the Lord stopped him and began to speak:

> "The nation of the United States over this next season is going to decline. You're going to see a decline, but it's going to be okay. It's

going to go through a time of darkness, but those that are in Me are going to be alright."

It was at that point that Joseph Z saw God's people coming back again in a different way. Through all they endure, the Lord is going to prepare and provide for His people, and it's going to be well with them.

Rick then shared how even during the worldwide flood of Noah, which to date is the most catastrophic event to ever take place, God protected and provided for His people. Similarly, even though we're living in destructive times, everyone who is in an ark of safety is going to be safe. Just as Noah and his family floated on top of the waters of destruction, so will we. The key is being obedient to what God tells us to do.

To be clear, we can't just do whatever we want to do or go wherever we want to go in these troubling times. Instead, *we must be led by the Spirit of God*. The safest place to be right now is where God leads you to be. If He sends you into the wildest war zone in the world or into some other place that seems illogical, go where He leads you. That's where you'll have peace, no matter what may be going on around you.

In 1991, God led Rick and Denise and their whole family to the former Soviet Union. For over 32 years they have lived in a land that was once dominated by atheism. Again and again, people have asked them, "Are you okay? Aren't you going to get out of there?" And Rick has always responded, "Why would I run from the will of God? **The safest place in the world is in the will of God**, and that's where we are."

Indeed, Rick and his family are a remarkable example of God's preserving power and His anointing to shine in the midst of darkness. The Moscow Good News Church, which Rick and his team planted, is thriving, and biblical teaching you can trust is being broadcast around the world from the RENNER Ministries TV studios in the city of Moscow, Russia. Praise God for His faithfulness!

God Will Provide for His Own

When we look back at times of great difficulty in the world, God has always provided for His people. Before the great famine struck, God raised up Joseph with a supernatural gift of administration and positioned him to oversee the harvesting and distribution of food. Four hundred years later, God delivered the children of Israel from Egyptian slavery, carrying the riches of their captors. Talk about a transfer of wealth! Every time God moved His children to the next phase of what they were called to do, He prepared them and prepared the way for them.

That is what we're stepping into — not just financial provision, but provision on every front. The Spirit of the Lord is making a way for many people where there seems to be no way. And those that have been hidden in darkness during times of normalcy are receiving supernatural strength to accelerate forward.

It's no accident that you are reading this study guide right now. God wants to speak to you in these moments and pour out His Spirit of might, wisdom, and revelation on you as you put your trust in Him — this is the Matthew 6:33 anointing. As you seek first the kingdom of God and His righteousness, everything you need will be added to you.

What kinds of "things" is God going to provide? They are food, clothing, shelter, and the necessities of life that unbelievers seek every day. And amid these dark, difficult times, their search for substance and how to be taken care of will drive them to God's people. Scripture says, "The Gentiles shall come to your light, and kings to the brightness of your rising. 'Lift up your eyes all around, and see: They all gather together, they come to you'" (Isaiah 60:3,4 *NKJV*).

Realize the anointing of God is on you and on all those that recognize the hour of the times in which we are living. We have the same anointing that the sons of Issachar operated in, and those that are lost without Christ are going to be drawn to that light in us. The Church will be a hub of security for the world that's struggling for its life.

Again, the Spirit of the Lord is speaking to you right now, and He wants you to know that He will make a way for you where there seems to be no way. Instead of there being a cry of "Ichabod" on the Body of Christ during this time, there will be an "Issachar" cry, and the Isaiah 10:27 anointing will break you out of bondage.

A Closer Look at the Anointing

Looking once again at Isaiah 10:27 (*NKJV*), it says, "It shall come to pass in that day that his burden will be taken away from your shoulder, and his yoke from your neck, and the yoke will be destroyed because of the anointing oil." The Hebrew word for "anointing" here is the same word for *fatness* or *muscularity for growth*. Thus, the anointing being described in this verse enables so much muscular growth that the person outgrows the yoke.

Now, when we talk about the anointing, we're talking about more than just warm fuzzies. In the context of Isaiah 10:27, it is actually talking about freedom from oppression — specifically governmental oppression that is lifted off the people incrementally until there is total freedom.

We saw in Lesson 1 that this verse describes three levels of anointing as well as three levels of breakthrough:

The first level of anointing is the *thirty-fold* level. It is when "the burden will be taken away from your shoulder." This is when you first begin to feel lighter and freer. But there's more freedom to be experienced.

The second level of anointing is the *sixty-fold* level. It is when the "yoke is taken away from your neck." In addition to feeling lighter, you have increased mobility and greater vision to see around you. Still, there's more freedom to be experienced.

Although many believers settle for a thirty- or sixty-fold level of freedom and anointing, it is not God's will for any of us to stay there. He wants us to go all the way and experience…

The level three anointing, which is a *hundred-fold* breakthrough. This is when "the yoke will be destroyed because of the anointing oil." This is complete liberation that enables you to do all that God has called you to do.

In celebration of God's kindness and generosity, David praised Him saying, "You crown the year with Your goodness, and Your paths drip with abundance" (Psalm 65:11 *NKJV*). This is a picture of God's anointing just raining around us to such an extent that we're walking through puddles of it! This is a promise that Rick claims not only for him and his family, but also for everyone that is a part of RENNER Ministries.

Psalm 133 also talks about the anointing and its direct connection with being in unity. In the *New Living Translation,* it says:

> **How wonderful and pleasant it is when brothers live together in harmony!**

> **For harmony is as precious as the anointing oil that was poured over Aaron's head, that ran down his beard and onto the border of his robe.**
>
> **Harmony is as refreshing as the dew from Mount Hermon that falls on the mountains of Zion. And there the Lord has pronounced his blessing, even life everlasting.**

Here we see Aaron, the high priest of Israel, standing in a puddle of anointing. This is also a picture of the Church. The anointing is on Jesus, who is the Head of the Church, and it comes down His beard and flows throughout the entire Body of Christ. God's plan is for us to stand drenched in a puddle of His anointing. That is the level of anointing that destroys the yoke of bondage and empowers us with freedom in every area of our life.

We Need the Reforming 'Spirit of Elijah'

Not too long ago, a well-known team of researchers conducted a study and determined that about every 20 years or so God releases a powerful revelation — or a "now word" — through a certain leader for their generation, and it begins to change everything. Initially, that revelation often inspires deep devotion to God and great passion among His people, and before long it turns into a movement.

Unfortunately, as time progresses, these movements become institutionalized within about 20 years. Leaders begin to circle around the revelation and build a new norm of values and culture, resulting in a more rigid, formulaic set of ideas and guidelines that lack passion. Although this is not necessarily bad, what we really need is for new life from the Holy Spirit to be continually breathed into us, so we don't become stale, stagnant, and void of fresh revelation.

This idea of becoming institutionalized doesn't just apply to the Church — it is true of all established institutions, such as businesses, corporations, universities, hospitals, humanitarian efforts, manufacturers, parachurch ministries, churches, and even families. We all need new revelations — a "now word" — flowing into our respective fields to keep things fresh, relevant, and effective. Hence, we need reformers.

Churches and ministries that become institutionalized are those that have lost their passion. Rather than function as a vibrant pipeline of God's power and restoration, they become merely a business. This is what has happened to many denominations that were once a blazing fire of Spirit and truth.

Much like the Early Church, what we need today is a return of the spirit of Elijah. Before Jesus came the first time, John the Baptist was sent to prepare the way of the Lord (*see* Matthew 3:1-3; Luke 1:13-17). God tells us through the prophet Malachi, "Behold, I will send you Elijah the prophet before the coming of the great and dreadful day of the Lord. And he will turn the hearts of the fathers to the children, and the hearts of the children to their fathers…" (Malachi 4:5,6 *NKJV*).

This activity of turning the hearts of the fathers to the children and children's hearts to their fathers describes a generational merging that breaks people out of the detached, unhealthy roles they've been function-ing in and become accustomed to. In other words, the reforming "spirit of Elijah" in God's people will breathe a "now word" that's full of life into institutions on all levels.

The major challenge for most reformers is the resistance to change from people within the institutions. Whatever the institution cannot control, it will begin to persecute and even attempt to kill. Thus, it is the job of a reformer to continue to stand up, speak life-giving truth, and refuse to hold on to offenses. Persistence empowered by the Holy Spirit will cause institutions to rightsize.

Stay Flexible in the Father's Hands

In order to be able to receive fresh revelation from God, we must remain flexible in the Father's hands. Jesus said it this way: "No one puts new wine into old wineskins; otherwise the [fermenting] wine will [expand and] burst the skins, and the wine is lost as well as the wineskins. But new wine must be put into new wineskins" (Mark 2:22 *AMP*)."

New wine represents fresh revelation and a fresh move of God. The wine-skin is our lives — specifically our hearts. To stay a "new wineskin," we must always aim to keep our hearts soft and pliable in the Lord's hands. When a church, ministry, organization — or an individual — institution-alizes the revelation they received from God, they begin to become an old wineskin. This means instead of being pliable, teachable, and open to new things, they become rigid, hardened, immovable, and set in their ways.

Just as oil kept wineskins soft and flexible, the oil of the Holy Spirit keeps us pliable and receptive to the new things of God. You don't have to become an old wineskin, but if you find yourself in that condition, there is a way to be renewed. Back in the day, for an old wineskin to be refurbished, it had to be beaten, thoroughly cleansed, and reconditioned with fresh oil. This rigorous process is also a picture of us being renewed. If you see that you have a hard heart, pray, *Lord, please forgive me for becoming hard-hearted and set in my ways. I desperately need You to soften my heart. Do whatever You have to do to make it tender, pliable, and sensitive to Your touch again. In Jesus' name. Amen.*

Fear NOT!

So many of us fear the future, and sometimes we even fear what we know God has called us to do. Yet if we really knew what the Lord had for us in its fullness, we just might not be intimidated. In fact, we might just press in even harder.

Friend, God is calling you into a deeper, richer, more vibrant relationship with Him than you've ever had before. His Holy Spirit is urging you not to be afraid or to shrink back. He's going to walk with you all the way to the end, so you don't have to fear the future. You have a Proverbs 31 anointing on you. You are clothed in scarlet, which represents the precious blood of Jesus, and He's going to take you through everything in front of you. It's going to be okay. All the pain you've been through will be redeemed, and your heart will be fully restored to the point that it is well with your soul.

In Jesus' name, we release a mighty spirit of faith and boldness over you right now — an empowerment from God that crushes anxiety, worry, panic, and fear in all forms. May His anointing come upon you and equip you with supernatural confidence and wisdom so that you can look at the future and know that Jesus is Lord, and you and your family are going to be okay. Be blessed in every way in Jesus' mighty name. Amen!

STUDY QUESTIONS

> **Study to shew thyself approved unto God, a workman that needeth not to be ashamed, rightly dividing the word of truth.**
> **— 2 Timothy 2:15**

1. Remember how we talked about the differences between the 30-, 60-, and 100-fold anointing and breakthrough? How did Elijah's protégé, Elisha, position himself to receive the fullness of God's anointing? (Read Second Kings 2:1-11.)

2. Consistent repentance is one of the most powerful things we can do to stay pliable and flexible in God's hands. For example, take the story in Jonah 3:6-10. What group of extremely wicked people repented to God for their sin? How did He respond when they decided to humble themselves and repent?

3. Becoming a new wineskin after having become hardened and set in a specific way of doing things is difficult, but SO worth it. What does God promise to do for us when we humble ourselves, repent, and allow Him to change us? (*See* Ezekiel 36:26 and 27 and First John 1:9.)

PRACTICAL APPLICATION

**But be ye doers of the word, and not hearers only,
deceiving your own selves.
—James 1:22**

1. Many times, people talk about the last days with a tremendous air of fear and uncertainty, as if God doesn't have enough to take care of all His kids. Somehow, we think that some of us will "slip through the cracks." How does this lesson change your perspective of God's care and provision for you as His child?

2. Name one area of life where you feel God calling you to not give up at the 30- or 60-fold mark of anointing and freedom. Did you know that there was even more freedom to be had? Dream a little about what that freedom might look like, sound like, and feel like in real life, and invite the Holy Spirit to help you cooperate with His plan and desires for you so you can experience a complete, no-going-back breakthrough.

3. Be honest: In what areas of your life do you sense the Holy Spirit showing you that you've become stubborn or set in your ways, like an old wineskin? Is it in your perspective of younger believers? The way the Gospel is presented? Maybe the way you spend time with God? Whatever it might be, invite the Holy Spirit to soften and change your heart and give you new and improved spiritual vision. Then watch how He works in your life in amazing ways.

TOPIC

A Corporate Superpower

SYNOPSIS

When it comes to breaking hell's economy, there is only one corporate superpower that can pull it off, and the corporate superpower we're talking about is *the Church*. We are the Body of Christ, made up of many individuals, but collectively we are one in Jesus. Although a corporate anointing is God's will, it is not a given; it's something we must rise up to do together. The fact is, if we as the Body of Christ ever unlock what is available to us, we will become the number one superpower in the world.

The emphasis of this lesson:

Hell's economy cannot prevail against the Church. It is the restraining force holding back evil on the earth. When we — God's called-out ones (His *ekklesia*) — globally unite and function in our gifts, we become the unstoppable corporate superpower that drives back the gates of hell.

What Is the 'Church'?

All throughout the New Testament, the word "church" is used, and it's the Greek word *ekklesia*. It's a compound of two words: the word *ek*, which is a preposition meaning *out* and where we get the word *exit*; and the word *kaleo*, which means *to call*. When we compound these words, the new word *ekklesia* describes *the called-out ones*.

What many people don't know is the word *church* didn't begin with the Bible. It was a secular term that originated in Athens, Greece. The *ekklesia* was a group of very distinguished people that had been elected and selected from society and called out to form a corporate body of leaders. This body of people was so powerful it made all the decisions for the city.

The New Testament writers and their First Century readers understood the meaning of the word *ekklesia*, which is why they used it to describe all of Christ's followers collectively. In their mind, the Church was not to be a little group of people huddled together in the corner of a dark room.

Instead, we're called out by God to be His distinguished people who rule and reign, setting the moral and spiritual agenda of cities, states, regions, and countries around the world.

The call of the Church is to be God's prophetic voice in the earth, and if we're not speaking His truth and setting the agenda, then we're missing our purpose. In Matthew 16:18 (*NKJV*), immediately after Peter got the revelation from the Father that Jesus is the Son of the Living God, Jesus said, "…On this rock," referring to the revelation, "I will build My church, and the gates of Hades shall not prevail against it."

To "not prevail against the church" means to not be able to overcome it. Hence, the gates of hell — which is the Luciferian, antichrist agenda and efforts — will not be able to successfully overcome the Church. Again, the Church globally coming together and doing what God called us to do is the unstoppable corporate superpower.

What Is the Church's Role Regarding the Antichrist?

As we mentioned previously, the "gates of hell" also refer to the world's systems. First John 5:4 (*NKJV*) says, "For whatever is born of God overcomes the world. And this is the victory that has overcome the world — our faith." The word "world" here is the Greek word *kosmos*, and it refers to *things that are organized and in order*. In this verse, it signifies *the organized systems of the world*. Satan is the god of the world's systems (*see* 2 Corinthians 4:4), and he masterfully manipulates everything through the spirit of antichrist, which is already in the world (*see* 1 John 4:3).

Now, some people have asked, "Is the Antichrist already here in the world today?" The truth is he could be here — we don't know for sure. It may be that he is hiding in the shadows waiting for the optimum time to take center stage on the world scene. What we do know from Scripture is that the Antichrist will not be revealed until that which is restraining him is removed. Paul wrote about this in Second Thessalonians 2:6-8:

> **And now ye know what withholdeth that he might be revealed in his time. For the mystery of iniquity doth already work: only he who now letteth will let, until he be taken out of the way. And then shall that Wicked be revealed.…**

Here, the Bible talks about the moment when the Antichrist will be "revealed," and this word is the Greek word *apokalupsis*. It is a compound of the word *apo*, meaning *away*, and the word *kalupsis*, which describes *something that is veiled, covered, concealed, or hidden*. When these two words come together to form the word *apokalupsis*, it depicts *the pulling back of a curtain or veil, exposing something that was formerly concealed or hidden from view*.

So what is *withholding* the unveiling of the Antichrist? Who is "he who now *letteth*?" Interestingly, the word "withholdeth" and "letteth" are the same Greek word — the word *katecho*. It means *to hold fast; to hold down; to hold back; to suppress; to restrain;* or *to hinder*. These words let us know that there is some supernatural force that has been restraining and holding back the forces of evil from fully taking control. Who has been on the earth since the time Paul wrote this and will be through the end of the age? It is *the Church*. Jesus declared, "…I will build my church; and the gates of hell shall not prevail against it" (Matthew 16:18).

This tells us how powerful the Church is. It is the restraining force against evil on the earth. When the Church is raptured, the Antichrist will suddenly be revealed, and it will take place "in his time" (2 Thessalonians 2:6). The word "time" here is the Greek word *kairos*, which signifies *a specific season* or *an opportunity*. The Antichrist is an opportunist. When the Church has been removed and the conditions in the world are just right, he will seize the opportunity and suddenly appear on the world's stage.

Again, the Antichrist may already be on the earth somewhere, but whether he is or not, the system of the antichrist — the gates of hell — are busily at work. During the Tribulation, after the Antichrist has been revealed and is dominating the planet, the book of Revelation says he will make war against the saints and overcome them (*see* Revelation 13:7). When we factor in Jesus' words in Matthew 16:18, we can see that this group of believers must be different than the Church (*ekklesia*) because Jesus said the gates of hell would not prevail against the Church.

How Has God Gifted the Church?

As son or daughter of God, you were born for something great. In fact, there is an assignment from Heaven that is uniquely yours in the time in which you live. Oftentimes, people get discouraged in life when they hear negative news stories that fill the airwaves. They are deeply affected by their environment and news of what's going on in the culture. But listening to reports of the scripted insanity being propagated by the spirit of antichrist is not what God has called His Church (*ekklesia*) to do. He has called us to know and understand who we are in Christ and to come together in unity.

The Bible says, "Each person is given something to do that shows who God is: Everyone gets in on it, everyone benefits…" (1 Corinthians 12:7 *MSG*). Indeed, the Body of Christ has been equipped by the Holy Spirit with a wide variety of amazing gifts.

- Romans 12:4-8 describes *seven motivational gifts.*
- 1 Corinthians 12:4-11 talks about the *nine manifestation gifts.*
- Ephesians 4:11 and 12 reveal the *five-fold ministry gifts.*

When we add all these gifts together, we see we have been given 21 fundamental gifts in the Church. There are others, but these 21 gifts show us the Body of Christ has been outfitted with a broad spectrum of giftings. When we — God's called-out ones (*ekklesia*) — stand up together and function as one in our gifts, we become the corporate superpower that drives back the gates of hell.

The reason we're not seeing greater effectiveness in breaking hell's economy is that many of God's people are trying to do other people's jobs. Each of us needs to recognize our own position and gifting in the Body of Christ and then get into the place God has called us to serve. Once we know our role and step into it, we can know how to support one another in our respective roles. This is what needs to happen to become a global corporate superpower called the Church. Working together in this way makes us unstoppable.

According to Psalm 133:3, this kind of unity commands the blessing of God on what we're doing. When God sees His children working together, He is so encouraged He begins to release economic blessing as well as supernatural healing on us and through us. First Peter 2:24 says that by Jesus' stripes (or wounds), we were healed. When God's people who are anointed with the gifts of healing are in the right place, healing power will flow. The right people in the right place with the right gifts will produce the right results.

When You Find Your Place, You Find Your Purpose

Rick shared how when he was younger in ministry, he often compared himself with others and tried to be like them. He would look at other ministers and think, *I don't walk like them. I don't preach like them, and I don't scream like them.* As a result of constantly comparing himself, he always felt inferior. Then one day, God brought him to the realization that uniqueness is what gives him a place in the Body of Christ. It was then that he stopped struggling to be like everyone else and fully embraced who God has called him to be.

When we as individual members of the Body of Christ find out who we're supposed to be and get in our place, that's when we really begin to make a difference. Additionally, when we come together and find our place with our tribe — those with whom God has called us to serve — our effectiveness grows exponentially.

How will you know you're with the right people? You will be well received by those with whom you're serving, not attacked by them. In other words, you can't say the wrong thing to the right people. A person who isn't in the right place is out of their lane, and when people are in the wrong lane, they are uninspired. That means they aren't functioning in their God-given anointing, and they're not flowing in His revelation knowledge.

Take for example the writing gift on Rick's life. The way God writes books through him is supernatural. Rick's part is to be disciplined, do the research, put in the time, and do the work. And then, when his preparation meets the opportunity, the anointing of God is released.

Let's say that once more and personalize it.

When *your* preparation meets God's opportunity — when you discipline yourself and do all you know to do to be ready for what God's told you to do — His anointing is released and begins to empower you to get the work done.

The thing that gets many believers in trouble is looking at a gift in someone else and thinking, *That's what I'm going to do, and that's where I'm going to go.* Sadly, this person has not heard from God — they've heard from themselves. Thus, they are uninspired and trying to achieve the results of one who is inspired in the wrong way. When a person forces or manipulates their way into a position God didn't call them to, they have no anointing or revelation to function in it.

The native tongue of the uninspired — those who are self-called, not God-called — is *criticism*. The uninspired are not truly where they're supposed to be, and therefore, they lack God's anointing and revelation. Think about the Pharisees and Sadducees during the time of Christ and the emerging Church. They represent the institution of religion that was critical of and cruel toward John the Baptist, Jesus, the apostle Paul, and countless others.

Like it or not, various levels of criticism, and at times cruelty, comes with the territory. Remember, whatever the institution cannot control, it has to kill or persecute at the very least. This is why it's vital that we rise up and unite, not fight. It's interesting to note that if the work is too small, men will fight, but if it's big enough for all, men will unite. God's calling men and women to unite as the Body of Christ and become a corporate superpower.

A Unified Church Is Like the 'Dew' of Mt. Hermon

How important is unity to God? To answer this question, we return to Psalm 133 where David wrote:

> **Behold, how good and how pleasant it is for brethren to dwell together in unity! It is like the precious ointment upon the head, that ran down upon the beard, even Aaron's beard: that went down to the skirts of his garments; as the *dew* of Hermon, and as the *dew* that descended upon the mountains of Zion: for there the Lord commanded the blessing, even life for evermore.**
>
> **— Psalm 133:1-3**

The word "dew" in this passage is talking about *the anointing of the Holy Spirit*. It is saying that the Holy Spirit in our lives is like "dew." To understand what this means, we must understand what dew is and how it functions.

There is moisture in the air all the time, but you can't see or touch it. It's invisible. However, when the atmospheric conditions are just right, and the air cools down to the "dew point," the moisture in the air condenses and begins to manifest as water droplets all over everything. These droplets of water are what we call "dew." Thus, the "dew point" is the point at which the air molecules become fully saturated with moisture and cannot hold another drop. Suddenly, the moisture in the air appears everywhere — on outdoor furniture, plants, trees, grass, everything. The moisture was there all along, but it didn't manifest until the right conditions were met.

When the Body of Christ comes together in unity, we create a spiritual "dew point." Suddenly, the tangible anointing of the Spirit is released on everyone. Think about the apostles and followers of Jesus. After being together for ten days in the upper room, they united as one, and as soon as they did, the spiritual dew point was reached, and the anointing of the Holy Spirit covered everyone there!

Unity is the spiritual *dew point* that triggers the anointing to manifest. This is the corporate anointing that God desires to give the Church, but He's waiting on us to unite and not fight. He wants to manifest His anointing on churches, ministries, denominations, cities, states, regions, and countries. Although we may not see or sense His presence in a concentrated way, He is there in our churches, our homes, and our lives. But He only manifests His presence where there is unity and peace. When we all get in our God-called positions and unite in Christ, anointing will be released on us like dew, empowering us to break hell's economy.

One reason people are suffering lack in the Body of Christ is because of incomplete teaching. Although there's been a lot of correct teaching, it's been incomplete. Take the subject of increase or prosperity, for example. For years it has been taught primarily for individual purposes, but a more complete teaching reveals that prosperity is meant to be a corporate anointing for the purpose of spreading the Gospel. So, whether it's health, wealth, increase, or overall effectiveness, when we come together corporately and are in the right positioning, we can change the world. That's what God's calling us to do in this time.

Be Aware of What Programming You're Receiving

When the Bolshevik Revolution took place around 1917, its leaders understood that to change a nation, they had to change its vocabulary. Accordingly, they began to redefine all the terms, and the citizens became very "woke." Moreover, the communist regime began pulling down all the old monuments and changing the very things at which people looked. They even created and appointed "thought police" because they

understood that to change the nation into what they wanted, they had
to control how people thought and the language they spoke. Authorities
began telling people what they could and couldn't say.

Meanwhile, Krupskaya, Lenin's wife, was appointed to oversee public
education. Her philosophy was, "You have to tell kids what you want them
to believe, whether it's right or wrong, and if you can form the thinking
of the kids, then you can take them out from under the authority of their
parents. At that point, you can build a new society."

All these efforts and more were put forth to reform the nation of Russia
and create a new generation, and it worked. This took place over 100 years
ago and is a vivid example of the gates of hell coming against people. It's
the same thing we are seeing repeated today in the Western world. As the
Bible says, "History merely repeats itself. Nothing is truly new; it has all
been done or said before" (Ecclesiastes 1:9 *TLB*).

Unfortunately, many people don't know history, which is why we see so
many today embracing socialism. That is not a system we need. It's godless
and driven by the spirit of antichrist — a spirit that is hungry for control.
This demonic entity has a thug-like intimidation mentality and tirelessly
tries to bully the culture, masquerading as a protective bodyguard.

This antichrist/thug spirit wants people to sit down, be quiet, and do what
they're told. Those who adhere to its demands suddenly begin to fall into
submission to the antichrist system. This spirit strives to make people feel
guilty about everything — even thinking their own thoughts. Ungodly
religion is very much the same way.

Jesus is the opposite in every possible way. He came and gave His life to
pay the price for our sins, and through faith in His finished work, we are
restored into right relationship with the Father. In addition to saving us
and setting us free from sin's power, God makes us His sons and daughters
and joint heirs with Jesus, sharing fully in His inheritance.

What has God called us to do? He's called us to be a light to the world
that is sinking into deep darkness. It's time to rise up, put on God's armor,
and stand against the thuggish antichrist spirit that wants to intimidate
us into being silent. We need to turn off the legacy news media that is
trying to tell us how to think and what to believe and arm ourselves with
truth. If we're ready to speak it in love, the Holy Spirit will open doors of
opportunity to speak.

'We Have One More Round'

As the teaching wrapped up, Joseph Z shared what he felt the Lord has been speaking strongly to his heart. He said: "I know the Spirit of the Lord is with us, and I really believe He's saying we have one more round. One more round means, 'If My people who are called by My name will humble themselves, and pray and seek My face, and turn from their wicked ways, then I will hear from heaven, and will forgive their sin and heal their land' (2 Chronicles 7:14 *NKJV*). If we'll seek God like He's told us to, He'll give us another season to stand and bring the Gospel to a dying world."

This prophetic word goes along with the words of the prophet Joel, which was quoted by Peter in Acts 2:17 and 18:

> **And it shall come to pass in the last days, saith God, I will pour out of my Spirit upon all flesh: and your sons and your daughters shall prophesy, and your young men shall see visions, and your old men shall dream dreams: And on my servants and on my handmaidens I will pour out in those days of my Spirit; and they shall prophesy.**

We're believing for the greatest outpouring of God's Spirit the Church has ever witnessed — beyond anything anyone has ever imagined. The preview of what's coming is happening now. As the darkness accelerates, so will the light of God's glory. We — the Church — are the secret weapon God is going to spring on the world!

Now, maybe you're thinking, *Well, what can I do? How do I stand up against this culture? The future is scary.* Friend, the Bible says, "For God has not given us a spirit of fear, but of power and of love and of a sound mind" (2 Timothy 1:7 *NKJV*), and "…Greater is he that is in you, than he that is in the world" (1 John 4:4).

It's time for you to really begin depending on God. He's going to break loose His economy into your life, and His favor is on you. James 1:17 says, "Every good gift and every perfect gift is from above, and cometh down from the Father of lights…." By His grace, you can learn to look at the enemy's antics and laugh at him just like God (*see* Psalm 2:4).

Know that He is with you, and you don't need to be intimidated for one second. Jesus is Lord, and your future is so bright! Even on a bad day, you're called to be the very best there is!

STUDY QUESTIONS

Study to shew thyself approved unto God, a workman that needeth not to be ashamed, rightly dividing the word of truth.
— 2 Timothy 2:15

1. When you read the definition of *ekklesia*, did it surprise you that it wasn't originally a religious or church-related term? Which Old Testament ruler can you think of that is a stunning example of what it means to be called out, equipped, and set apart for a purpose to bring about godly change?

2. Remember how we talked about the importance of each person discovering and embracing what they've been called and equipped to do? What happens when we spend all our efforts trying to do someone else's job? And what happens when we learn to delegate the right tasks to the right people? Consider the examples in Exodus 18:13-23 and Acts 6:1-7. What is the Holy Spirit showing you in these passages?

PRACTICAL APPLICATION

But be ye doers of the word, and not hearers only, deceiving your own selves.
— James 1:22

1. Scripture says *faith comes by hearing* (*see* Romans 10:17). In other words, what we hear again and again, we begin to believe — whether true or untrue. Mainstream media is a perfect example of this principle. How do you think mainstream media has affected you personally? What does this lesson show you about the power of intentionally keeping truth before you in what you watch and listen to?

2. God has designed and equipped each one of us *on purpose* to be an influencer for His kingdom and to shine His light in a dark world. But in order to live this out, we each need to know and fully embrace the calling He's placed on our life. Do you know what your calling is?

In what field (or fields) or areas do you have the gifting and passion to make a difference?

3. In what specific ways have you embraced your calling and begun to develop your gifts and skills? Take time to pray and invite the Holy Spirit into the process, asking Him to help you more fully walk out your purpose. You'll find more joy than you ever thought possible right in the center of His will for you.

TOPIC

A Future Without Babylon

SYNOPSIS

What does it mean to *break hell's economy*? Again, we're talking about breaking or defeating a system. Right now in the world, we are witnessing a collision of systems or a collision of kingdoms. The kingdom of darkness — aka the gates of hell or hell's economy — wants to overcome you and everyone else in the world, but we know if you're a believer, that can't happen. God's Word says in First John 4:4 (*NLT*):

> **…You belong to God, my dear children. You have already won a victory over those people, because the Spirit who lives in you is greater than the spirit who lives in the world.**

And it also says in First John 5:4 (*NLT*):

> **…Every child of God defeats this evil world, and we achieve this victory through our faith.**

Jesus has made a way for us during these days of difficulty, giving us opportunities to advance and take territory. Indeed, crises create opportunity, and the times we're living in only qualify for more opportunity. The truth is, as the people of God we have exactly what we need to live and do what God has called us to do (*see* 2 Peter 1:2). What we're lacking is a revelation of what we have, and that is what this series (and the book) *Breaking Hell's Economy* is about. In this lesson, we will look at a very real possibility of what could be and what our part is in seeing that potential future unfold.

The emphasis of this lesson:

When we talk about Babylon, we're talking about the satanically controlled system of hell's economy. God wants His people to break free from this system and adhere to the economics of His Kingdom. Rather than dominate or take over society by force, we're called to be influencers of our culture on all levels. His corporate anointing will be released on the Church as we each know our role, find our place, and celebrate with our tribe.

Understanding 'What Could Be'

There are many future events that the Lord gives us in advance as a sneak peek. These include events like wars, rumors of wars, famines, plagues, earthquakes, and worldwide deception (*see* Matthew 24:4-7). Yet there are other specific things that Jesus would like to see happen but are not guaranteed. One of the things Joseph Z shared that the Holy Spirit has been speaking strongly to him is *what could be*.

An example of *what could be* is seen in what Jesus said when He came into Jerusalem toward the end of His ministry. He said, "O Jerusalem, Jerusalem, the city that kills the prophets and stones God's messengers! How often I have wanted to gather your children together as a hen protects her chicks beneath her wings, but you wouldn't let me" (Luke 13:34 *NLT*). At another time, Jesus voiced what He would like to see when He returns to earth: "Nevertheless, when the Son of Man comes, will he find faith on earth?" (Luke 18:8 *ESV*).

These were things Jesus desired to see and what could be, but what actually takes place is indicative of whether we are obedient to do what God's given us to do. In other words, our willingness to obey what He's said is a major factor that decides what will take place.

God Wants His People
To Break Free From 'Babylon'

One very specific thing that the Lord is calling us to do is to thrive and break free from Babylon. What do we mean by "Babylon"? Again, we're talking about hell's economy or a system — a system of the world that started in Genesis 11 with a narcissistic leader named Nimrod, the son of Cush and grandson of Ham, Noah's son. The name "Nimrod" basically means *we rebel*, which is exactly what he led the world to do.

It seems Nimrod, the rebel, instigated and oversaw the building of a large tower in the land of Shinar. The Tower of Babel, as it became known, was a type of ziggurat — a rectangular stepped tower — that was constructed by many civilizations at that time. Although the tower was likely tall, its real purpose was more spiritual in nature. Many agree this tower was built to be an interdimensional, spiritual portal, which would enable the people of Earth to visit another realm — a realm in which fallen angelic beings were waiting for permission from mankind to infiltrate the world with their sinister schemes.

Keep in mind, God had specifically instructed the people to be fruitful and fill the whole planet (*see* Genesis 9:1). The fact that Nimrod defied God's command and corralled everyone in one place was outright rebellion, and "…Rebellion is as the sin of witchcraft…" (1 Samuel 15:23 *NKJV*). Just as rebellion in the natural is a defiance of natural authority, so witchcraft is a defiance against spiritual authority. What was unfolding at "Babel," which can be translated as *the gate of the gods*, was a creation of unauthorized access into the spirit realm for the ultimate purpose of interacting with evil powers.

Sound familiar? Today we have that same system of rebellion operating in the Twenty-First Century. Of course, the CERN project may come to mind, but the overall ousting of God from the public square along with the embracing of humanism and the rapid rise of the occult and even Satan worship are all signs that the Babylon spirit is alive and well on planet Earth. This system of rebellion is powerfully impacting the way people think — and therefore act — in every arena of life.

The Babylon system operates through what the Bible calls *mammon*, which is the love of money. Again, the devil doesn't have the anointing of God's Spirit, so he seeks to control people and the systems of the world through economics and commerce. By influencing the way people think regarding finances and material goods, Satan seeks to control culture and take it where he wants it to go. It's no wonder God said, "For the love of money is the root of all evil…" (1 Timothy 6:10).

To be clear, Satan uses the spirit of mammon to create a love of and need for money and possessions instead of a love and need for God. Friend, it's time for us to break free from this Babylonian system, which is hell's economy, and align ourselves with what Jesus said in Matthew 6:33 (*NKJV*): "But seek first the kingdom of God and His righteousness, and all these things shall be added to you." Remember, "The blessing of the Lord makes one rich, and He adds no sorrow with it" (Proverbs 10:22 *NKJV*).

Is There Such a Thing as a Transfer of Wealth?

Some people ask, "Does the Bible say there will be a transfer of wealth from the hands of the wicked to the righteous in the last days?" Well, Proverbs 13:22 (*NKJV*) does say, "…The wealth of the sinner is stored up for the righteous," but this promise is conditional, not automatic. Always keep in mind that it takes the whole Bible to make a whole and complete Christian. Being obedient in fulfilling what God has called us to do and honoring Him with our giving is key to experiencing His blessings. A person who is disobedient, lazy, and stingy toward God shouldn't expect an overflow of His blessings to suddenly show up at their door.

When we look at God's Word, there really is a wealth-transfer precedent that can be seen throughout its pages. If you think about it, the Exodus was one of the greatest wealth transfers that ever took place in history. What's interesting about this story is the people of Israel worked in captivity and slavery for hundreds of years, and they were never appropriately paid. However, when they left Egypt, God made sure they were compensated for all the years they were cheated out of their wages, and they left loaded.

That said, we need to point out one major mistake believers make, and that is believing prosperity or breaking out of hell's economy is just for them *individually*. Yes, it's true that God wants each of us to prosper and be in health, even as our soul prospers (*see* 3 John 2), but there's more. The corporate blessing — when we come together as the Church in unity and God pours out prosperity — that's the greatest form of a wealth transfer that can take place.

We see a picture of this corporate anointing of prosperity in Isaiah 60:1 and 2 (*NKJV*):

> **Arise, shine; for your light has come! And the glory of the Lord is risen upon you.**

For behold, the darkness shall cover the earth, and deep darkness the people; but the Lord will arise over you, and His glory will be seen upon you.

The fact that darkness is covering the earth and deep darkness is covering the people describes a time of severe crisis. It's in such times when divine opportunities appear. Ultimately, when darkness is dominating the earth and the people, it's because the revelation of God's truth is missing. This denotes a full-scale, all-out assault by the gates of hell.

Oh, but friend! Light shines brightest in the darkest of night. When hell has overplayed its hand, the glory of the Lord shows up and arises on us, His Church. Look at what Isaiah 60:3 and 5 (*NKJV*) say:

The Gentiles shall come to your light, and kings to the brightness of your rising.

Then you shall see and become radiant, and your heart shall swell with joy; because the abundance of the sea shall be turned to you, the wealth of the Gentiles shall come to you.

Notice it says, "the Gentiles shall come to your light," and "the abundance of the sea shall be turned to you." The word "sea" throughout Scripture often refers to *the nations* or *the sea of humanity*. Likewise, the word "Gentiles" indicates *the unsaved people of the world*. Thus, unbelievers from all nationalities and walks of life will turn and come to you — first, for the light of the Gospel, and second, because you will possess the wealth that they seek. These things are what will draw the lost to God's people.

If we couple this passage in Isaiah 60 with Matthew 6:25-34, we discover a life-changing truth. Here Jesus repeatedly tells us not to worry about what we'll eat, drink, or wear because worrying about and seeking after these things is what the Gentiles do. They're in bondage to the system of Babylon — hell's economy. If we'll put God first and seek Him and His will first, He'll provide our every need (*see* v. 33). He knows what we need before we ask, and He will not withhold one good thing from anyone who is diligently seeking Him! (*See* Psalm 84:11.)

We're Called To Be Influencers

What does God want us to be? We are to be *influencers* of society. There are many good-meaning Christians who believe we are to take over all the various areas of culture — and even do it by force if necessary. This is not God's way. Although many aspects of "dominion theology" and a "kingdom-now" mindset sound great, they're not in keeping with the heart of God.

To be clear, God has not called Christians to take over society and dominate in some military way. He doesn't force us to love and serve Him, and therefore, He doesn't want us to force others to love and serve Him either. Instead, what He desires is for genuine believers to steward seats of influence well in areas of government, business, entertainment, science, education, healthcare, the Church, and every other place of authority and influence in culture.

Many people in Scripture exhibited this kind of influence. We see it in the life of Abraham, whose reputation influenced the kings and leaders of surrounding nations. Likewise, Joseph was an influencer, too. God prepared and positioned him in Egypt so that when the famine came, he was equipped to save millions of lives and break hell's economy over the civilized world of that day. Then there was Moses, Mordecai, Esther, Deborah, and so many others who used their influence to literally shape the course of history. Like these people of God, we're called to shine our light of influence to the point that even commerce and society are affected in great ways. As we do, God will work through us to draw all mankind to the light of Jesus.

Influence is what is required to shine the light of the Gospel. This includes seeking first God's Kingdom and righteousness, and all these things being added unto you. It also requires us as believers to seriously consider if we are where we're supposed to be. If we're not where God has called us to be, doing what He's gifted us to do, it's going to drastically affect not only our lives but the lives of so many others. Every believer must passionately seek the Lord like his life and destiny depend on it — because they do.

As God's people, we can't just pick up and move somewhere solely because it has a more glamorous job opportunity, better amenities, or a more comfortable climate. Before we make a move, we need to stop, drop, and pray. If the Spirit of God wants us to stay put, He'll make it clear. If He's moving us somewhere else, the Bible says He'll lead us out by *peace* and *joy* (*see* Isaiah 55:12). Those who are where God has placed them, doing what He's called them to do, are positioned for blessing. Simply put, the empowerment of the Gospel will go around the world completely paid in full when each member of the corporate Church is positioned where God has called us to be for the days ahead.

This concept of wealth transfer doesn't mean every single person is going to be a multimillionaire or billionaire. It simply means that as believers are where God has called them to be and doing what He's called them to do, they will experience overflowing abundance and be able to accomplish their mission with joy. And at the same time, they will push back the gates of hell. Again, this wealth transfer is *what could be* — if we are obedient to God and believing for it.

Know Your Role…Find Your Place… Celebrate With Your Tribe

We saw in Lesson 3 that the Body of Christ has been thoroughly equipped by God to continue and carry out the ministry that Jesus began. Through Peter, God instructed us to "serve one another with the particular gifts God has given each of you, as faithful dispensers of the magnificently varied grace of God" (1 Peter 4:10 *J.B. Phillips*). What kinds of gifts have we been given?

- **seven motivational gifts** (Romans 12:4-8)
- **nine manifestation gifts** (1 Corinthians 12:4-11)
- **fivefold ministry gifts** (Ephesians 4:11,12)

Altogether we have 21 fundamental gifts in the Church. The fivefold ministry gifts of apostles, prophets, evangelists, pastors, and teachers are the governmental gifts, and the remaining 16 gifts make up the primary positions for the rest of the Body of Christ. When all the parts of the body are where they're supposed to be and doing what they're called to do, we are collectively anointed by the Holy Spirit to be a corporate super-power — God's *ekklesia* — that drives back the gates of hell.

If we really want to break hell's economy and drive the devil crazy, what we need to do is begin celebrating each other's wins. Imagine what would happen if members in the Body of Christ celebrated and applauded fellow members who received a breakthrough. Heaven only knows the cata-strophic damage that would be done to the kingdom of darkness. Wow!

It's God's desire that you find yourself surrounded by others who *celebrate* — not tolerate — each other's giftings and blessings. These individuals are your spiritual "tribe." If you see a fellow member get a promotion or receive extraordinary favor, rejoice! A win for another believer is a win for you, too. If you sense envy, jealousy, or greed trying to enter your heart, pray and ask the Lord for grace to reject it and sincerely celebrate their victory. Remember, we are all on the same team and in the same line, and as you rejoice when others are blessed, you could very well be next!

Are you beginning to see the importance of really knowing your part and your place in the Body of Christ? Are you grasping how vital it is for you to be a part of a vibrant church and attend regularly? (*See* Hebrews 10:25.) The enemy doesn't stand a chance against a believer who has a revelation of what God really wants for them.

Remember, you can't say the wrong thing to the right people. You'll know you're with your tribe when you're *celebrated*, not just tolerated. Indeed, there's indescribable power in finding and uniting with your "tribe" — being and serving alongside like-minded people. God commands a blessing on such corporate unity. You will benefit, they will benefit, and everyone will be positioned to receive a God-ordained wealth transfer that benefits the entire Kingdom.

Beat the System

Second Corinthians 4:4 (*NLT*) says, "Satan, who is the god of this world, has blinded the minds of those who don't believe. They are unable to see the glorious light of the Good News...." We have noted that the word "world" in this verse doesn't describe the earth or planet. It is the Greek word *kosmos*, which depicts *something that has order*, and in this verse, it describes *the organized systems of the world*. This includes the systems of education, entertainment, fashion, world markets, finances, and the courts. Thus, *Satan is the god of systems*. When we talk about breaking hell's economy, we're talking about breaking the world systems of the enemy.

Think about the system — or world — of fashion. Can you see the enemy's influence there? How about the world of entertainment, which seems to grow darker by the day? Then there's the judicial system, which has countless members who've been hijacked and weaponized to do the devil's bidding. Even the education system has been harnessed by the enemy to indoctrinate our children in the kind of thinking that will pull them away from Christ. The same is true of the fields of science, medicine, and others…yet there is still hope. God has called and equipped us, His people, to begin to regain what the enemy has stolen in these arenas.

How do we effectively put a stop to his schemes? Through prayer, proclaiming God's Word, and becoming influencers in these world systems. Jesus said that we're to be a *light* in darkness and the *salt of the earth* (*see* Matthew 5:14,15). Light enables us to see, and salt preserves, adds flavor, and even promotes healing. As light and salt, our presence changes things. Again, this doesn't mean we're called to take over society. It just means we're called to influence our culture on all levels. No one person can do everything, but each of us can do something to make a difference. As we submit our lives to God, He will use us to restore and change the world systems and rescue the perishing.

Friend, that is the purpose of the wealth transfer — to get the Gospel around the world. The Bible says, "And you shall remember the Lord your God, for it is He who gives you power to get wealth, that He may establish His covenant which He swore to your fathers, as it is this day" (Deuteronomy 8:18 *NKJV*). Here we see the source of wealth is God, and the purpose of wealth is to establish His covenant, which means to see people saved. Yes, God wants us to be blessed personally, but the big picture — and the real purpose — is to preach the Gospel to the ends of the earth, and then Jesus will come.

Trust God…
Stand and Speak Truth

Now, many people today are afraid — including many Christians. As a result, they've inadvertently made this statement: "I guess it's come to this; we're just going to have to believe God and do what we believe." Surprisingly, this careless statement is filled with truth. We *do* have to believe God and act on what we believe.

The great news is nothing that is happening in the world is a surprise to God, and He's not nervous or afraid. Actually, part of the shaking in the world is coming directly from Him. He said in Hebrews 12:26 (*NLT*), "When God spoke from Mount Sinai his voice shook the earth, but now he makes another promise: 'Once again I will shake not only the earth but the heavens also.'" Why all the shaking? "…So that only unshakable things will remain" (Hebrews 12:27 *NLT*).

It's interesting to note that the name Antipas was used in New Testament times, which in Greek means *against everything*. Unbelievers viewed and labeled Christians as *Antipas* — people who were against everything in the world. "Oh, they're just so narrow-minded and bigoted," they likely said. And because Christians appeared to be against everything, the Gentile world ostracized them and treated them like outcasts.

We see many believers being treated the same way today. Maybe you've experienced such treatment yourself. If so, be encouraged. You're in good company! Friend, this is not a time for us to cower in silence. We need to stand up and speak the truth in love without fear of being criticized or canceled — even if the world doesn't like what we say. As Joel Renner says, "To be clear is to be kind." If we truly love people, we need to clearly tell them the truth.

A Closing Prayer

As we conclude this lesson, we want to include the prophetic prayer Joseph Z prayed over everyone who joined in the teaching:

In the name of Jesus, I speak life and victory over every person. God hears your prayers, especially for your children and grandchildren. Your face has come up clean before Him, and He deeply loves you. He's going to take your kids up in His hand, and you will see a turn in their life even this year and even during a stormy time.

Your prayers are not going unanswered; God hears you. He sees all those that have pain in their body, and I speak strength over you right now and say, 'Be healed in the name of Jesus!' God is touching you and giving you a breakthrough.

I come against the spirit of fear and the spirit of antichrist trying to intimidate you and cause you to be anxious. I cut that off your life right now. You don't have to be afraid or shrink back. For the Lord God Almighty has called you to increase and abound in this season, and He'll deliver you from this present evil age as He promised in Galatians 1:4.

Indeed, God is delivering you and setting you free. He's breaking hell's economy over your life and family right now and in no way wants you to lack or be in fear. He is the Great Provider, and your life matters. Jesus loves you, and He's drawing you out of darkness into the light right now. On a bad day, you're called to be the best there is. In Jesus' name. Amen!

STUDY QUESTIONS

**Study to shew thyself approved unto God, a workman that
needeth not to be ashamed, rightly dividing the word of truth.**
— 2 Timothy 2:15

1. The love of money and the pursuit of worldly possessions won't serve
    us well in this life or the one to come, and Lot's life is a perfect exam-
    ple. Where did he and his family move because of a lure for wealth and
    earthly possessions (*see* Genesis 13:7-13)? According to Genesis 14:1-16,
    what happened to Lot and his family, and what did his uncle Abraham
    have to do as a result? Where did Lot choose to go after this
    intervention (*see* Genesis 19:1)? How did Abraham come to his rescue
    (*see* Genesis 18:16-33)? In the end, what happened to Lot and his family
    (*see* Genesis 19:12-38)?

2. Being in the right place at the right time with the right people is vital.
    What do these passages repeatedly say about receiving direction from
    God? (*See* Psalm 25:8,9,12; 32:8; 48:14; 73:24; Isaiah 30:21.) What
    do Colossians 3:15, Isaiah 55:12, and Romans 14:23 identify as inter-
    nal signs or confirmations that the Holy Spirit is leading you?

3. In these last days, God says, "The Gentiles shall come to your light,
    and kings to the brightness of your rising" (Isaiah 60:3 *NKJV*). What
    does First Peter 3:15 say you're to do to be ready when unbeliev-
    ers come to you? If you had about a minute to share how God has
    changed your life, what would you say? (Also consider the Gospel
    encapsulation in Titus 3:3-7 and First Corinthians 15:1-4).

PRACTICAL APPLICATION

**But be ye doers of the word, and not hearers only,
deceiving your own selves.**
— James 1:22

1. Remember the "dew point" we learned about in Lesson 3? What did
    those facts tell you about the power of being in *godly* unity with other
    believers (as opposed to ungodly unity, like Babel)? How would you
    hope to see God move in your church? In your community? In your

family? Ask Him to help you come together to create that spiritual "dew point" and experience His manifest presence and power in a dynamic, new way.

2. On that same note, how does knowing that your presence and gifts should be *celebrated* and not just tolerated affect your view of relationships? Take a moment to pray and invite the Holy Spirit to give you greater discernment to help you know who your God-given tribe is, and the ability to be that kind of brother or sister to those He places in fellowship with you.

3. Sometimes a scarcity mentality, jealousy, and greed can creep into our thoughts so quietly that before we know it, there's bitterness poisoning our relationships. Do you ever find it hard to celebrate others' wins? If you do, there's a good chance it's rooted in a painful memory that God wants to heal. Bring it to Him, ask for His grace to grow, and watch the envy fade away. Remember, you're in the same line for blessings, and God's heart is to bless you in amazing ways. So keep clapping for others until your turn comes.

TOPIC

Breaking Hell's Economy Off Your Family

SYNOPSIS

God is all about family. He is our Heavenly Father, and as believers in Christ, we are His sons and daughters (*see* 1 John 3:1,2). To experience all the blessings He has planned for our lives, obedience is required. The Bible says, "If you are willing and obedient, you shall eat the good of the land" (Isaiah 1:19 *ESV*). Your obedience to God — even in the small things — will work to break hell's economy off you and your family and unleash a supernatural chain reaction of God's blessing.

The emphasis of this lesson:

Being obedient to what God tells you to do will help break the enemy's influence off you and your family. When you do something in the natural in obedience to God, He'll do something supernatural in the spirit. If you'll do the difficult, He'll do the impossible. Your persistent obedience in the natural will break hell's economy in the realm of the spirit.

The Enemy Is After Our Children

One of the most prominent areas that the spirit of antichrist is attacking right now is the next generation. In unprecedented ways, the enemy is attacking people's children and grandchildren — especially in the area of their identities. This thug spirit is carrying out its nefarious agenda by assaulting the minds of our youth. Slowly but surely, he's been stealing and redefining basic words in perverted ways so that wrong is called right and what is right is called wrong.

Working through the world systems of education, entertainment, and even the courts, the enemy has sought to modify this generation's thinking by getting them to throw away the tried-and-true beliefs of previous generations and adopt a new worldview. Even now, there are children who are so deceived that they're fighting their own family members to defend the demented philosophies of this age.

For example, recently there was a story on the news of a woman that was denied the right to adopt a child because she wouldn't sign a paper stating that she would be willing to give hormone-altering drugs to the child to enable him to change his gender. That's both wrong and deeply heartbreaking, and many people are experiencing these kinds of situations right now.

History shows that the moral meltdown in America began to happen with the removal of prayer from public schools on June 25, 1962. This was followed by the removal of Bible reading in schools in 1963 (Abington Township v. Schempp) and then the removal of the Ten Commandments in 1980 (Stone v. Graham). The enemy has been working hard to steal this country's spiritual legacy from future generations ever since.

All this is ultimately the spirit of antichrist, and his efforts have become more and more intense. What started out slow has turned into a rapid freefall of demoralization. Things are unfolding so rapidly now, it's hard to keep up with everything. This situation has left many believers scratching their heads saying, "What in the world are we supposed to do?"

What Can We Learn From Cornelius' Life To Protect Our Family?

To help us know how we can stand against this evil spirit that is attacking our families, we turn to the book of Acts and the story of Cornelius, a Roman centurion of the Italian Regiment. Although this man was a Gentile and pagan to the bone, the Bible says he feared God, prayed, and gave generously to the poor (*see* Acts 10:1,2). God was so touched by Cornelius' actions that He sent an angel to him telling him to send for the apostle Peter, who would then tell Cornelius what to do.

Meanwhile, the Spirit of God prepared Peter's heart to go to Cornelius' home with the message of the Gospel. When Peter arrived, Cornelius took him inside and shared what had happened.

> **…Four days ago I was fasting until this hour; and at the ninth hour I prayed in my house, and behold, a man stood before me in bright clothing, and said, 'Cornelius, your prayer has been heard, and your alms are remembered in the sight of God. Send therefore to Joppa and call Simon here, whose surname is Peter. He is lodging in the house of Simon, a tanner, by the sea. When he comes, he will speak to you.' So I sent to you immediately, and you have done well to come. Now therefore, we are all present before God, to hear all the things commanded you by God.**
>
> **— Acts 10:30-33 (*NKJV*)**

With all eyes on Peter, he began to share the gospel message, but while he was still speaking, the Holy Spirit showed up and fell on Cornelius' entire household. In one fell swoop, everyone was baptized in the Holy Spirit (this is what some refer to as the Gentile Pentecost). Cornelius and his whole household were the first recorded Gentiles to receive Christ and His Spirit!

Don't miss this: the reason all the family members — including the children, grandchildren, friends, and servants — had the opportunity to be saved and filled with the Spirit was because of Cornelius' obedience. He had a reverential fear of God, he was a giver, and he obeyed the Lord's instructions. He did what he knew to do to pursue God, and God's grace met him and his family where they were. By his faith and obedience, Cornelius broke hell's economy off his family!

This is a biblical example we can follow. Obedience to what the Lord instructs you to do will break hell's economy off your family. As a father, mother, or grandparent, your decision to obey God can push back the gates of hell. If He asks you to move somewhere, move. If He asks you to go somewhere or attend a certain church, do it. Likewise, if God asks you to pray a certain way or give a certain amount, do whatever He prompts you to do. Yes, there may be something about that act itself, but most important is your obedience — it's how you submit yourself to God and resist the devil so he will flee from you (*see* James 4:7).

And you never know what kind of a domino effect will take place as a result. Whenever you obey God, it starts a chain reaction that will lead all the way to your entire family being born again, which is God's heart and greatest desire.

How Did Joseph and Mary Break Hell's Economy Off Their Family?

When we think about parents who stood in the gap for their kids, Mary and Joseph, the parents of Jesus, come to mind. We know from the account in Luke 1 that the angel Gabriel appeared to Mary and told her that she had found exceeding favor with God. Out of every woman who would ever live, Mary was selected to give birth to Jesus, the Son of God. Rather than resist or reject the opportunity, she accepted it and walked in obedience to God's instructions.

At that time, Mary was betrothed to be married to Joseph. When Mary became pregnant by the Holy Spirit during their engagement period, Joseph could have legally divorced her and put her away. But when God sent an angel to speak to Joseph and urge him to take Mary as his wife because she was indeed pregnant with God's Son, Joseph chose to obey God's instructions.

What happened when they followed the voice of God? Jesus, the Son of God, was born into the world. Through faith and obedience, Joseph became the foster father of Jesus and began raising Him as his own. About two years later, the Magi showed up, bringing Jesus an extraordinary caravan of riches that was fit for a King. Joseph and Mary's obedience broke hell's economy off Jesus — even off the financial limitations that would have hindered Jesus' ministry. This gift from the Magi to Jesus was a divine wealth transfer like no other.

Think about it. During Jesus' ministry, He never publicly received an offering. Using the resources He had been given, He reached the multitudes *and never had to ask for money*. Because He always kept the Kingdom of God first, everything Jesus ever needed always showed up, and His blessed life began with Mary and Joseph's obedience. They broke hell's economy off Jesus and off their family, and it had a domino effect on all mankind.

Friend, God wants to reach our families and break hell's economy off our lives. He wants to sever the antichrist system of Babylon off us. Again, how do we do it? We obey God.

Obedience in the Natural Produces a Supernatural Reaction

There's a powerful principle found in First Corinthians 15:46. Here, the apostle Paul wrote, "…The spiritual is not first, but the natural, and afterward the spiritual." In context, this is talking about Adam and Jesus; Adam, the natural man came first, then Jesus — the Last Adam — came, who is the life-giving Spirit. Still, there's a vital principle here that we need to grasp.

When you do something in the natural in obedience to God, He will do something in the realm of the spirit. What He asks you to do may be difficult to obey, but if you do the difficult in the natural, He'll do the impossible in the realm of the spirit.

For example, if you physically lay your hands on someone who's sick and pray for their healing out of obedience to God's Word (*see* Mark 16:18), God will ultimately bring about their supernatural healing by His Spirit. Likewise, if in obedience to God you give financially to someone, God will bring you a supernatural blessing by His Spirit. Similarly, if you open your mouth in the natural and speak to someone about Jesus, God will begin to open their eyes spiritually to see their sinful condition and God's perfect love for them and their need for Jesus to be their Savior and Lord.

It's really the law of sowing and reaping (*see* Galatians 6:7,8). You must take action by faith in the natural to get a supernatural reaction. In other words, whatever God has instructed you to do — through His Word or by

His Spirit — keep doing it. Keep speaking His Word, keep forgiving and praying for those who mistreat you, keep loving the unlovely and walking in humility, and on and on the list goes. Your persistent obedience in the natural will break hell's economy in the realm of the spirit.

A personal example from Joseph Z's life. Several years ago, the Lord asked Joseph and his wife, Heather, to step out of active ministry and sit for a season and just listen to what He was saying to them. At the time, they were very busy building a ministry, broadcasting messages, and doing many other things. Nevertheless, Joseph felt the Lord say, "If you'll rest for a season and sit for a few moments with your family, I will bless all of you."

This was a very hard thing to do, but he knew in his heart he had heard from God. When he did in the natural what God asked him to do, he found that it placed his family in a completely healthy place. This demonstrates that there's always grace to help you do what is hard — but that doesn't mean it's not hard. Surrendering in obedience to do what God asks us to do releases His grace to do the difficult.

When you finally surrender in obedience to do what God has told you to do, it becomes easier because His grace shows up, and you work with the empowerment of His Spirit. For many, this may look like going to or staying at a particular church where you are having challenges with people — including those in leadership. But if you'll stay where you believe God wants you to be, He'll give you His grace to do it and bless you for your obedience.

Rick shared this story from his life. He said, "Being in the right place at the right time with the right people, doing what God told you to do, is very important and produces a supernatural chain reaction of blessing in your life. In fact, I will tell you what I believe is the secret to the success of my ministry. It's not because we're so smart; it's simply because we did what we were told.

"I remember one day I stopped what I was doing, and I asked the Lord, 'Why did You choose me? With all the things I know about myself, why would You choose me?' And I heard Him say, 'Because I knew you would do what I asked you to do.'" Friend, when you do the natural part, the supernatural part always shows up. When you obey what God tells you to do — especially in connection with your family — you will break hell's economy off all your lives.

Prophetic Words of Prayer for Your Life

As this final lesson began to wrap up, Rick asked his guest, Joseph Z, to pray for everyone who was joining them in this series. With the Holy Spirit's leading, Joseph Z then spoke a series of prophetic words that we have captured in the paragraphs that follow. May the Holy Spirit speak and minister hope, healing, and direction to you personally as you reflect on these words:

"I sense so strongly that there are people who have been having struggles in your family. Some members may have left your sphere of influence — maybe children, grandchildren, or someone close to you. The world's voice has been very strong in your household, but God wants to break your family free from the world's influence. Just as it's not your desire that your family serves the world, neither is it God's. I also sense strongly that it's not His will that they leave home.

"Right now, I believe the Lord wants to remind you that He'll never leave you nor forsake you, and His hand is going out at this moment to work on your behalf, in the name of Jesus. I take authority over every circumstance that has driven children and grandchildren toward the world and away from their families. We send out laborers into the harvest field right now to draw them back. Satan, how dare you touch the Lord's anointed and come against these families. Back off, in Jesus' name.

"We release God's strength over you and call your children home, in Jesus' name. And we call them back into the relationship and service with the Lord God Almighty. He's not going to leave them or forsake them.

"I also sense that someone just had surgery, and I'm watching it right now. You went through a surgical procedure, and at the end of it, you began to feel stress and turmoil over your family. And the Lord is saying to you, 'I am going to intervene on your behalf right now, today.' So, in Jesus' name, I declare there will be phone calls and there will be restoration.

"There's going to come a time of justice and shaking in the United States specifically. When that happens, expect your phone to ring, expect goodness to come, and expect God to use what darkness is trying to manifest against you. He'll use it for the good of the family and to bring people out of darkness and into light. It won't all be bad, believe me; God's going to use the wickedness to bring light to pass and release life into your household.

"I also see that the spirit of antichrist has tried to bring a heavy weight and burden over many of you, and the Lord is saying, 'Don't fall for it, and don't shrink back! This is your greatest hour! On a bad day, you're called to be the best there is.'

"I see someone right now who has an issue while you're driving. You get stressed out when you're driving because you're thinking about what's going on in the culture and what's happening around you. And the Lord is saying unto you, 'Draw near to Me, and I will draw near to you.'

"I also see a banker and a banking scenario. There's going to be strength over this banking scenario; God's going to work out the narrative for how to manage resources and be an adviser to a greater capacity. I see you working out things for non-profit organizations and helping people in a greater capacity. There's going to come a second wind for this 501(c) (3) narrative; I see something with this right now where God's going to begin to help people and begin to bring in new wisdom and a new force of legal power that will stand up for the Church in this next year. I see strength and victory coming with that. A spirit of might is going to break this thug intimidation spirit off your family and off your children. The Holy Spirit is roaring for victory in your house.

"Someone has a cooking business, and you're going to step up with cooking. You're going to begin doing things that have to do with culinary arts, and you're going to be doing things as a service for people. And the Lord says, 'I'm putting prosperity on that; there will be a "hot sauce" on that. And it's going to bring strength up for many,' in the name of Jesus.

"Many of you are going to get a revelation that your business is your ministry, and you're going to see God touch people through it, in Jesus' mighty name.

"I also hear the words *Social Security*. And the Lord is saying unto you, 'I am your Social Security; I am your Provider. I will make a way where there's been no way.' Even in the middle of darkness, when the world goes down, get ready to go up, because God has called you and marked you, and this is your finest hour. If you do the difficult, which is simply obeying God, God will do the impossible. This is your greatest day and your greatest hour; God has called you at this time.

"I also have a sense that the great merging is here. God is going to begin to bring many of you together in unlikely alliances, and some people you thought you would never work with — people you thought were from the other side of the tracks, so to speak — God is going to unite you with.

"If it's too small, men fight, but if things are big enough, men unite. And I see God bringing a great uniting, a merging in the culture where many will come together and stand as a united front. I also see the Lord bringing a spirit of forgiveness and grace between people. You're going to experience this in many of your relationships — the spirit of love, grace, and forgiveness is going to lead and guide you in this next season. And the merging will happen, and that is how God will use your life to break out of hell's economy. I see victory coming for people."

Just before closing the teaching, Rick spoke this prophetic word as he prayed:

"Friend, I particularly feel that some of you have children and grandchildren that have hooked up with the wrong person in a relationship, and it's broken your heart. But they're going to come home, and what's going to surprise you is that when they come home, they're going to bring that person with them.

"So, it's not just going to be one person who comes back home, but two. Two are going to come back to the Lord — and maybe even more. The devil has tried to take your loved one down, but the end result will be a harvest of people coming to Christ. God is going to move; I saw that while Joseph was ministering.

Lord, we agree with what Joseph prophesied and ministered — that every wandering person would wake up. We know You don't do evil things in anyone's life, yet we pray that through the events they've experienced, they'll wake up and say like the prodigal son, 'What in the

*world am I doing here when I could be home?' And Lord, may they
come running home and bring their friends with them. The devil will
be sorry for what he did because he's not going to lose one; he's going to
lose several in the process. In Jesus' name. Amen!*

STUDY QUESTIONS

**Study to shew thyself approved unto God, a workman that
needeth not to be ashamed, rightly dividing the word of truth.
— 2 Timothy 2:15**

1. Through this lesson, what did you learn about the power of obedience
   in Cornelius' life? How about in Mary and Joseph's life? How did
   their obedience connect their family closer to God and set them up
   for success?

2. Obedience, which is following God's instructions, is crucial to breaking hell's economy over our lives. Read Judges 6:25-32 and tell what
   the Lord instructed Gideon to do to purge his family's home. Has the
   Lord given you any specific instructions regarding praying for your
   family and purging your home of the enemy's influence? If so, what
   has He told you to do? Have you obeyed Him?

3. Carefully read God's instructions to Joshua and Israel regarding their
   victory over Jericho in Joshua 6:17-19. Then read the story of Israel's
   defeat at the city of Ai in Joshua 7:1-12. How did one man's sin affect
   the nation's ability to stand against the enemy? What did God tell
   Joshua he (and Israel) needed to do with the things "devoted" to destruction? What is the Holy Spirit showing you about your own life and family through this story? Are you holding onto anything that is weakening
   your ability to stand and defeat the devil? What actions do you sense
   the Holy Spirit is asking you to take? (If possible, read this story in the
   Amplified Classic version.)

PRACTICAL APPLICATION

**But be ye doers of the word, and not hearers only,
deceiving your own selves.
—James 1:22**

1. What's one way that the enemy tried to come against you as a child?
   How did it affect you? This can be a hard thing to remember and

think through, but when you ask the Holy Spirit (and even other believers you trust) to walk with you, it will be one of the most healing things you'll ever do. Journal what the Holy Spirit shows you, invite Him to do what only He can do, and watch the freedom and breakthrough that come in your life as a result.

2. The legacy of breaking hell's economy over your life and your family is for all of us, whether we have children or not. When you cooperate with God's work in you and see the enemy's influence in your life obliterated, that victory transfers to everything and everyone you influence, including coworkers, friends, spiritual kids, and even strangers you interact with every day. What's one thing you want to see your children, your grandchildren, and the people in your sphere of influence free from? Begin to pray against the enemy's influence and invite the Holy Spirit to connect all your loved ones in a closer, more intimate relationship with Jesus. Remember God is working, so keep your eyes open for evidence in your life and theirs that hell's chains are BREAKING, in Jesus' name!

NOTES

Rick Renner's guest during this series is Joseph Z, founder of Z Ministries. Joseph is an international prophetic voice who builds lives by the Word of God in the church, government, and marketplace. He and his wife Heather currently reside in Colorado Springs, CO, with their two children. For more information, visit **josephz.com**.

Joseph Z. *Breaking Hell's Economy: Your Guide to Last-Days Supernatural Provision.* Shippensburg, PA: Harrison House Publishers, 2022.

Notes

Notes

CLAIM YOUR FREE RESOURCE!

As a way of introducing you further to the teaching ministry of Rick Renner, we would like to send you FREE of charge his teaching, "How To Receive a Miraculous Touch From God" on CD or USB format.

In His earthly ministry, Jesus commonly healed *all* who were sick of *all* their diseases. In this profound message, learn about the manifold dimensions of Christ's wisdom, goodness, power, and love toward all humanity who came to Him in faith with their needs.

☑ YES, I want to receive Rick Renner's monthly teaching letter!

Simply scan the QR code to claim this resource or go to:
renner.org/claim-your-free-offer

R renner.org

f facebook.com/rickrenner • facebook.com/rennerdenise

youtube.com/rennerministries • youtube.com/deniserenner

instagram.com/rickrrenner • instagram.com/rennerministries_
instagram.com/rennerdenise